# Soul of Rome

**A GUIDE TO THE 30 BEST EXPERIENCES**

WRITTEN BY CAROLINA VINCENTI
PHOTOGRAPHED BY SOFIA BERNARDINI AND CLAIRE DE VIRIEU
ILLUSTRATED BY CLARA MARI

JONGLEZ PUBLISHING

Travel guides

*"THERE IS ONLY ONE ROME IN THE WORLD. HERE I FEEL LIKE A FISH IN WATER ..."*

GOETHE

Rome: Travel instructions

Taking on Rome is no easy task: there are too many layers, too much history, too many monuments. Rome, the Eternal City by definition, eludes any simple attempts at classification; there are so many (too many) stories, images, tales. That's why we created this guide through a process of elimination, choosing only those fragments of the city's soul that, in our opinion, have resisted the uniformity of globalisation and mass tourism. At the same time, how can anything remain secret in a place that has been explored for centuries? So, starting from the premise that no other metropolis has played such a central role in history over the last 2,500 years, we sifted through the present in search of traces of character that have crystallised in the city's spaces. In writing about them, we let ourselves be guided by our hearts, avoiding simply compiling a list of addresses.

Rome used to be where you went to forge an education by exposing yourself to the experiences of life and knowledge that we call culture. Pilgrims sought the soul of the place in the sacred, while laymen sought it in the profane; but both went into raptures about the stones, churches, and palaces.

Yet, in reality, the soul of Rome, then as now, is to be found in its contradictions. A popular and patrician city, forever bountiful and generous: like the colonnade of Saint Peter's welcoming children in its embrace; the meanderings of the Tiber encircling the domes of the historic centre; and the narrow winding streets preceding the oval of Piazza Navona, the city's Baroque lounge. A "magical and poisonous city" (in the words of the poet Valerio Magrelli), it continues to offer itself to us in all its greatness and decadence. A place of idleness *par excellence*; an idleness extolled by the ancients, as it happens.

What we have tried to do is write about the experiences you can have in its streets and alleyways, strolling Roman-style, allowing yourself to be blinded by the sun on its terraces, or abandoning yourself to the pleasures of its cafés, where Romans read the papers with the nonchalance of those who have lived through so many centuries and know that everything passes.

The Romans have every cuisine in the world at their fingertips yet they prefer to surrender to the joys of *pasta carbonara* in a dark alley, or *grattachecca* (ice shaved from a block on demand and flavoured with pieces of fresh fruit) from a kiosk on the banks of the Tiber, just like a hundred years ago.

We like to think that the places in our guide will strike a chord with travellers, allowing them to gather fragments of authentic Roman life from these small islands where the city's ancient and future soul is still offered up for the taking.

Carolina Vincenti

# WHAT YOU WON'T FIND
## IN THIS GUIDE

- directions to the Colosseum
- hop-on hop-off open-top bus stops
- touristy trattorias near the Trevi Fountain

# WHAT YOU WILL FIND
## IN THIS GUIDE

- aphrodisiacal spaghetti carbonara
- where to enjoy a glass of wine on the street, surrounded by locals
- how to sleep in a cardinal's bed
- rare herbs from the Roman countryside
- Caravaggio's barber
- the Vatican Museums before the crowds get there
- the world's oldest road you can cycle along
- a secret speakeasy
- the pope's socks

# THE SYMBOLS OF
## "SOUL OF ROME"

Less
than €10

€10
to €40

More
than €50

First come,
first served

Make
a reservation

100%
Roman

Opening times often vary,
so we recommend checking them directly
on the website of the place you plan to visit.

# 30 EXPERIENCES

# GO BARGAIN-HUNTING
## AT THE AMATEUR FLEA MARKET

It's a real pleasure to wander around the flea market of Borghetto Flaminio (also called the Rigattieri per Hobby – *rigattiere* means 'second-hand goods dealer'), just a few steps from Piazza del Popolo. This is where, every Sunday, after having gone through their wardrobes during the week, the capital's upper middle class rent a table to sell the clothes they no longer wear.

You'll find a whole lot of vintage items and sometimes luxury brands (ties, handbags and even table linen, sheets or cufflinks) in a friendly and rather 'hobbyist' atmosphere.

Over the years, the two owners, Paolo Tinarelli and Enrico Quinto, have amassed one of the richest collections of Italian clothes from the late 1950s – they breathe new life into them by taking them on travelling exhibitions around the world.

The beautiful National Etruscan Museum of Villa Giulia is just a stone's throw away.

**RIGATTIERI PER HOBBY**
**PIAZZA DELLA MARINA 32**

+39 06 5880 517     mercatidiroma.com/mercati-delle-pulci-e-vintage/111-borghetto-flaminio     Entrance fee: €1.60

# THE BARBER
## OF CARAVAGGIO

Rome has as many barbers as a Rossini opera, but some are more special than others, including these two:

> SALA DA BARBA GENCO
It's said that at the foot of the Torre della Scimmia, Caravaggio, who lived nearby, got into a fight with a barber boy. The place still exists; Sala da Barba Genco is now the city's oldest barbershop. In addition to classic cuts, Roberto, the nephew of founder Silvano Rossi, offers his "Genco shave" – 50 delightful minutes, involving rose water, argan oil, calendula cream, and more.

**SALA DA BARBA GENCO**
**VIA DEI PORTOGHESI 17**

+39 06 686 9881                    gencosaladabarba.com

### > GIUSEPPE CERRONI ACCONCIATORE

For those who speak Italian, Giuseppe Cerroni can take you on a true journey back in time to the golden years of Cinecittà. After starting out as an apprentice to Dino de Laurentiis's barber, and as Silvana Mangano's hairstylist, he went on to style the hair of most of the actors and directors of the 1960s: Ferreri, Comencini, Guttuso, Pasolini, and Moravia, who wouldn't devote more than four minutes to his beard while Elsa Morante waited impatiently for him ...

What has stayed with Giuseppe from those years are endless anecdotes and an inimitable know-how. His speciality is a scalp massage, ideally rounded off with hand (up to the elbow) and foot (up to the knee) treatment.

**GIUSEPPE CERRONI ACCONCIATORE**
**VIA GIAMBATTISTA VICO 44**

+39 06 361 1465

# A DOLCE VITA-STYLE
# ROMAN WARDROBE

At Sartoria Ripense you can enjoy the luxury of ordering a bespoke suit created specially for you by masters of the ancient art of tailoring. The handmade menswear at this store, as well as at Camiceria Mattioli and Albertelli's, has just the right touch of classic, timeless elegance.

Le Tre Sarte, an atelier run by young craftswomen just a stone's throw from Piazza Navona, makes fabulous unisex waistcoats and colourful women's dresses, painstaking work that manages to combine tradition and modernity ... at affordable prices.

PHOTO CREDIT: SARTORIA RIPENSE

**SARTORIA RIPENSE**
**VIA DI RIPETTA 38**

+39 06 3233 727
info@sartoriaripense.com
sartoriaripense.ecwid.com

**CAMICERIA MATTIOLI**
**VIA DELLA STELLETTA 30**

+39 06 6873 359

## - VALERIO MAGRELLI -

POET

### Is Rome still poetic?

Yes, in spite of itself. Sometimes I'm amazed when I notice certain buildings or certain streets where the city's millennial stratification is powerfully revealed. I ask myself how it's possible that so many different people managed to create so much beauty without consulting with each other. In Rome, the urban planning sometimes seems to have developed entirely on its own, in a coherent and necessary manner, as autonomously as a botanical miracle.

### Where else do you still see traces of the soul of the city?

It's pointless to give in to nostalgia, but of course it's still lovely when you happen on an artisanal boutique that has survived the tidal wave of Irish pubs and Bengali catch-all shops. While Rome's historical problem lies in its management, it's surprising to discover places or practices that are managing to resist the brutal commercialisation that came to a head with a chariot-racing project at Circus Maximus. You might as well just bring the lions back to the Colosseum, as long as you replace the ancient Christians with the current administrators.

### A poetic motto?

"Magical and poisonous", a definition of Rome taken from the travel diary of Jean-Paul Sartre that seems to me to sum up perfectly the feeling of a millennia-old metropolis as sublime as it is detestable. Not many have expressed so succinctly the oxymoronic, contradictory, irremediable nature that contrasts the sublime vertigo of the city's places with a population oppressed by centuries of theocracy. I don't think anyone can hate the Romans more than someone who was born in Rome.

### Which poetic text about the city do you think deserves to be better known?

Italy has a tremendous poet who isn't well known at all, even though he was admired by contemporaries of his such as Goethe and Stendhal: Giuseppe Gioachino Belli, whose sonnets are absolute 19th-century masterpieces.

Belli represents a poet world – perhaps the only one who was capable of merging so absolutely with the beloved-hated city that accommodated him; a material and metaphysical poet who is most similar to the English poet John Donne.

# SPEND A NIGHT
# IN THE MOST BEAUTIFUL
# VILLA IN ROME

It's one of Rome's most amazing secrets. The exquisite Villa Medici offers the privilege of staying in two historic suites which were apartments of the Medici family.

When we say privilege, we mean it: after dinner, as you enter the villa through the small door cut into the large central doorway, you immediately feel you're experiencing something exceptional.

In the silence of the night, go up the villa's wide travertine stairs to the famous gardens.

PHOTO CREDIT: DANIELE MOLAJOLI

**VILLA MEDICI**
**VIALE DELLA TRINITÀ DEI MONTI**

Reservations by e-mail only and no more than four months in advance: standard@villamedici.it

Specify that you wish to stay in a historic room (classic rooms, also located in the villa, are available at considerably lower rates)

The two rooms (some 70 square metres – each!) feature 16th-century frescoes by Jacopo Zucchi and coffered period ceilings. They either offer views of the marvellous gardens or 180-degree views of Rome. In the beautiful Salon Lili Boulanger, in front of one of the bedrooms, there's a piano. In 2023, the guest rooms and the Boulanger Salon, along with three other historic rooms of the Villa Medici, were given a modern touch by designer India Mahdavi.

N.B: These rooms don't come with luxury-hotel amenities or services: there's no elevator or staff to carry your luggage, and breakfast isn't served. But the experience is unforgettable ...

**#05**

# TRADITIONAL ROMAN CUISINE
## WITH A CREATIVE TWIST

You're in the heart of the tourist centre but want to avoid the usual scams? Just a stone's throw from the Pantheon, in a picturesque little square in the historic centre, Grano is a very pleasant restaurant that serves the great traditional Roman dishes – *pasta alla carbonara*, *aglio e olio* and *all'amatriciana*, for example – but with a welcome creative twist to switch things up a bit.

The owners, Danilo Frisone and Saverio Crescente, also run Cresci, a restaurant with a small bakery not far from St Peter's Basilica, which supplies Grano with its excellent bread. Two safe bets, both in areas generally overrun with tourists.

PHOTO CREDIT: EMANUELA RIZZO

**📍 GRANO**
**PIAZZA RONDANINI 53**

**📍 CRESCI**
**VIA ALCIDE DE GASPERI 11–17**

+39 06 6819 2096
ristorantegrano.it

+39 06 5184 2694
cresciroma.it

# DISCOVER
# **CONTEMPORARY ROMAN COOKING**

In its stylish contemporary decor, Retrobottega offers high-quality cooking that relies almost obsessively on the irreproachable quality of its ingredients. Prepared right before the customer, the dishes change each week.

Near the counter demarcating the open kitchen are two convivial tables, each for ten people.

P.S: Retrobottega also has a special pasta workshop and a bar with wines from small producers. Here, once a week, you can eat wild salads foraged by the staff in the Roman countryside, and other goodies.

PHOTO CREDIT: RETROBOTTEGA

**RETROBOTTEGA**
**VIA DELLA STELLETTA 4**

retro-bottega.com

**Pasta workshop: Retropasta**
Via della Stelletta 4
+39 06 6813 6310

**Wine bar: Enoteca Retrovino**
Via d'Ascanio 26a

PASTA

# ON THE QUEST FOR
## ROME'S BEST ICE CREAM

Don't be fooled: in Rome, long waiting lines are not always a guarantee of quality. To find the best ice cream in town, follow this simple advice: for chocolate meringue ice cream and fruit sorbets, trust San Crispino; for the best tiramisu and chocolate flavours, try the Gelateria del Teatro; and for pistachio, Otaleg (that's *gelato* – 'ice cream' in Italian – backwards) and Günther Gelato Italiano are safe bets..

For a seat outside, head over to Pica (the rice pudding and wild strawberry ice creams are superb!) and Palazzo del Freddo, located behind Piazza Vittorio, with its stunning 1930s decor.

📍 **GELATERIA DI SAN CRISPINO**

Via della Panetteria 42
Piazza della Maddalena 3
ilgelatodisancrispino.com

📍 **GÜNTHER GELATO ITALIANO**

Via dei Pettinari, 43
gunthergelatoitaliano.com

📍 **GELATERIA DEL TEATRO**

Via dei Coronari 66
gelateriadelteatro.it

📍 **OTALEG**

Via di S. Cosimato 14a
otaleg.com

📍 **PALAZZO DEL FREDDO GIOVANNI FASSI**

Via Principe Eugenio 65
gelateriafassi.com

📍 **GELATERIA ALBERTO PICA**

Via della Seggiola 12

# ESCAPE THE CROWDS
# **IN AN EXCEPTIONAL PALACE**

When the crowds in the streets, on the piazzas and in the churches and restaurants of Rome are a little too overwhelming, there is a solution for those who cherish silence and tranquillity: the fantastic Altemps Palace located right in the heart of the city.

Interestingly, although the palace and its collections are truly exceptional, the palace itself is empty most of the time.

Wander joyfully among the antique statues up to the beautiful loggia on the first floor. Make sure not to miss the Grande Ludovisi sarcophagus (3rd century AD).

**PALAZZO ALTEMPS**
**PIAZZA DI SANT'APOLLINARE 46**

museonazionaleromano.beniculturali.it | Entrance fee: €10

# Sant'Eustachio
## il caffè

# #09

# THE ULTIMATE
## ESPRESSO

OK, so it's not exactly a secret. But if you're hankering after the ultimate espresso, then head over to Caffè Sant'Eustachio, right around the corner from the Pantheon.

You might have to wait in line, but, while you do, watch the baristas in action behind the coffee machine. You'll probably notice that their hands are hidden by a barrier: the technique used to prepare Caffè Sant'Eustachio's speciality, *doppio cremoso* (double creamy), is in fact a secret. Don't worry though – *'cremoso'* doesn't mean there's any milk or cream involved; this espresso is simply so exceptional that it's almost like cream of coffee ...

📍 **CAFFÈ SANT'EUSTACHIO**
**PIAZZA DI S. EUSTACHIO 82**

+39 06 6880 2048                    santeustachioilcaffe.it

# A GUIDE TO
# **COFFEE-DRINKING**
# **IN ROME**

*Cappuccino*

CAPPUCCINO: coffee blended
with frothy steamed milk.
Italians drink it at breakfast
or in the course of the morning
but never after meals.

*Caffè al vetro*

CAFFÈ AL VETRO: espresso served
in a glass so you can also
appreciate its colour.

*Caffè ristretto*

CAFFÈ RISTRETTO: a more
concentrated espresso
made with less water.

**Granita**

GRANITA: a Sicilian recipe
made with coffee and half-crystallised
ice topped with whipped cream.
Perfect for summer.

**Macchiato**

MACCHIATO: espresso
with a touch
of cold milk foam.

**Corretto**

CORRETTO: espresso infused
with a small shot
of *grappa* or *sambuca*.

**Caffè schiumato**

CAFFÈ SCHIUMATO: espresso
capped with a dollop
of hot milk foam.

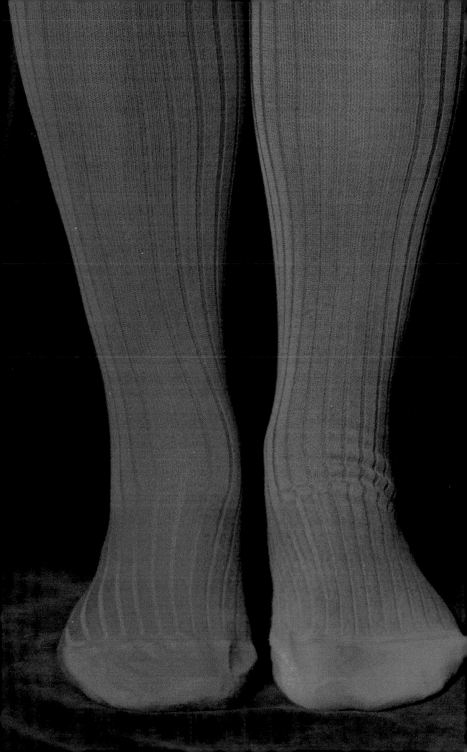

# BUY SOCKS LIKE
## **THE POPE'S**

Founded in the 1790s, Gammarelli has been famous in Rome since 1798. For six generations, Gammarelli – and Gammarelli alone – has been dressing the pope.

In addition to cassocks and other clothing reserved for the clergy, Gammarelli also sells exceptional socks, coloured for maximum impact.

So there really is nothing to discuss; simply ask them to open the sock drawers for you so you can choose a crimson or bright red pair … and nothing else, just like the pope. They're perfect for wearing discretely (or not) at home, or as a gift for very select friends.

**DITTA ANNIBALE GAMMARELLI**
**VIA DI SANTA CHIARA 34**

+39 06 6880 1314

gammarelli.com

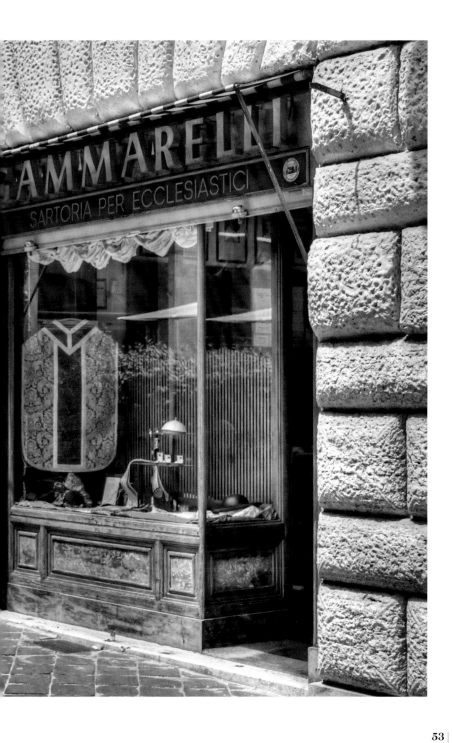

# A ROOFTOP
# STRAIGHT OUT OF A DREAM

It's worth making a reservation to secure your spot on Rome's most gorgeous rooftop. From here – the fifth floor of Palazzo Doria Pamphilj, over the library of Pope Innocent X – the view of Piazza Navona, Borromini's Church of Sant'Agnese in Agone just a few metres away, and the rooftops of Rome in general is truly exceptional.

N.B. The restaurant's prices – in keeping with the location – are sky-high.

**TERRAZZA BORROMINI**
**VIA DI SANTA MARIA**
**DELL'ANIMA 30**

+39 06 6821 5459
+39 391 311 4523

terrazzaborromini.com/contatti

# CHILLING
# ON THE STREET
## WITH A GLASS OF WINE
## IN YOUR HAND

Il Goccetto, run by Sergio Ceccarelli – or Sergetto, as everyone calls him – is a mere stone's throw from the Farnese Palace. What makes it truly magical is that you can just take your glass of wine out with you onto the street. Which almost everyone does, since you're not likely to find any room inside …

Then just set down your cheese and meat platter on the bonnet of a parked car and strike up a conversation with your neighbours. The night is off to a good start.

**IL GOCCETTO**
**VIA DEI BANCHI VECCHI 143**

+ 39 06 9944 8583

# ROMAN-STYLE
# STREET FOOD
# IN CAMPO DE' FIORI

It isn't easy to figure out where to have lunch in the uber-touristy Campo de' Fiori without falling into a tourist trap.

Head over to the south-west corner of the square to Forno di Campo de' Fiori for some delectable *pizza rossa* (red pizza). Not really pizza at all, except in name (and dough), pizza rossa is a sort of sandwich with tomato sauce that you eat standing up, just like the locals – who flock to this Roman institution no less than tourists do.

Another pro: *pizza rossa* will set you back less than €1.50.

If you're really hungry and want to switch up your palate, try the *pizza bianca* (white pizza), which is available filled with mortadella, among other options.

📍 **FORNO DI CAMPO DE' FIORI**
**PIAZZA CAMPO DE' FIORI 22**

+39 06 6880 6662      fornocampodefiori.com

# THE ALLURE OF
# **THE *MARITOZZO***

In Rome, it's not the all-powerful croissant that rules but the *maritozzo*. In Papal Rome, this soft brioche of ancient origins, sometimes refined with raisins, was frequently given as an engagement gift to marriageable young women – hence the name *maritozzo*.

Surrounded by old-fashioned tarts and cakes, the *maritozzo*, topped with a cloud of whipped cream, is the not-to-be-missed speciality at this retro pastry shop.

What if savoury food is more your thing? Il Maritozzo Rosso, located in a picturesque corner of Trastevere, has brioches with seemingly infinite combinations of magical fillings.

**REGOLI**
**VIA DELLO STATUTO 60**

+39 06 487 2812          pasticceriaregoli.com

IL MARITOZZO ROSSO
VICOLO DEL CEDRO 26

€

+39 06 581 7363

ilmaritozzorosso.com

**More *maritozzi***
ROSCIOLI CAFFÈ PASTICCERIA
LARGO BENEDETTO CAIROLI 16

€

+39 06 8916 5330

rosciolicaffe.com

# HAVE DINNER
## AT A DELI

Just around the corner from Campo de' Fiori, with a decor that's a perfect cross between deli and trattoria, Roscioli is an obligatory stop for anyone exploring the flavours of Roman cuisine.

Using premium ingredients, Roscioli executes all traditional Italian and Roman dishes to perfection, including the famous *cacio e pepe* (pasta with cheese and pepper) and the even more renowned *pasta carbonara*: pasta, pecorino, a mix of exotic peppers, a touch of magic, and that's it.

PHOTO CREDIT: MAURIZIO CAMAGNA

**ROSCIOLI**
**VIA DEI GIUBBONARI 21**

+39 06 687 5287          info@salumeriaroscioli.com

# IN THE PUREST
# **ROMAN TRADITION**

A very warm welcome from the Palladino family (with Tonino at front of house and his daughter Raffaella in the kitchen) awaits you here. For top-quality traditional cuisine just a stone's throw from the Ghetto, you can't go wrong at La Vecchia Roma.

During the high season – in other words, most of the time – the peaceful terrace is perfect for enjoying countless specialities prepared with brio, including the delicious *bucatini all'amatriciana*.

**LA VECCHIA ROMA**
**VIA DELLA TRIBUNA DI CAMPITELLI 18**

+39 06 686 4604                    ristorantevecchiaroma.com

# BUY GROCERIES DIRECT
## FROM THE BEST
## LOCAL FARMERS

Taking our cue from the Romans, who know how it's done, we do our grocery shopping at the stalls in this convivial covered market just a stone's throw from the Circus Maximus and the Forum.

Every weekend, producers from the Roman countryside come into town to sell forgotten herbs, wild asparagus, freshly pressed olive oil, Roman chicory, winter artichokes and ancient varieties of fruits. At the back, in the open courtyard with a view of the historic centre, you can also sample dishes prepared in a friendly, down-to-earth atmosphere.

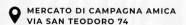

📍 **MERCATO DI CAMPAGNA AMICA**
**VIA SAN TEODORO 74**

+39 06 489 931

# ITALIAN SONGS
IN A PARK WITH
BREATHTAKING VIEWS

Amidst the pine trees on the Aventine hill, which offers a spectacular view of the city, you'll find the gorgeous Giardino degli Aranci (garden of the orange trees).

When the weather is nice – in other words, very often – singers regularly come here at sunset to croon old Italian tunes to the great delight of everyone present.

**GIARDINO DEGLI ARANCI**
**PIAZZA PIETRO D'ILLIRIA**

DAILY: from sunrise to sunset

**#19**

# TALKING TO ANGELS
## IN THE BASILICA OF
## SANTI QUATTRO CORONATI

Far from the usual tourist routes, in the district of Celio, the fortified basilica of Santi Quattro Coronati is one of the most charming churches in Rome.

We recommend visiting the church shortly before closing time to attend vespers sung by the nuns who live in the adjacent convent. In an atmosphere marked by deep contemplation, their voices echo below the vaults of the church and bring a real sense of peace.

Take a moment to admire the magnificent floor that underwent reconstruction work during the 11th century and is made of marble from the Roman Forums.

Before vespers, be sure to visit the monastery and admire the beautiful frescoes in the Chapel of Saint Sylvester. The wonderful cloister opens onto the nuns' chambers.

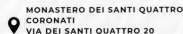

**MONASTERO DEI SANTI QUATTRO CORONATI**
**VIA DEI SANTI QUATTRO 20**

+39 06 7047 5427 | monachess4@gmail.com

Chapel of Saint Sylvester: accessible from the second courtyard on the right. Use the bell of the convent's anteroom

# GO FOR A RIDE
# **ON THE OLDEST ROAD**
# **IN THE WORLD**

A 20-minute car ride from the city centre, at the corner of Via Cecilia Metella, Caffè Appia Antica is where you should go to rent a bike or a horse to explore a section of the magnificent Via Appia, the oldest paved road in the world. Roam the Roman countryside on thousand-year-old lava-stone paving amidst villas and the ruins of gravestones that still slumber between the pine and cypress trees.

Give it a go on a Sunday, when the Appian Way is closed to cars.

 **APPIA ANTICA CAFFÈ BICI E CAVALLI**
**VIA APPIA ANTICA 175**

+39 06 898 7957 (landline) / +39 338 346 5440 (mobile)
info@appiaanticacaffe.it
appiaanticacaffe.it

To rent a horse, give Roberto a call:
+39 348 446 4094 (mobile)

# THE BEST PIZZA
## IN ROME

The 'Pizza Awards 2019' proclaimed Pier Daniele Seu the best *pizzaiolo* in Rome – and the eighth best in all of Italy. Far from offering the classic *margherita* or four-cheese pizza, Pier Daniele has set himself apart by venturing off the beaten track. Nothing is run of the mill at Seu Pizza Illuminati – especially not the pizza, which features a puffed outer crust (called *canotto* by the Neapolitans), a far cry from the Roman tradition, which favours a very thin crust.

So head over to this inconspicuous little street in Trastevere to try the *'fior di cotto'* pizza (squash blossoms, cream, *stracciatella* cheese, cooked ham, seawater and olive powder) or the vegetarian *'Basilicata* coast to coast'.

PHOTO CREDIT: BEATRICE MENCATTINI

📍 **SEU PIZZA ILLUMINATI**
**VIA ANGELO BARGONI 10**

+39 06 588 3384                  seu-pizza-illuminati.business.site

in pizza we trust

## 'PIZZA IS LOVE ...'

As Pier Daniele Seu puts it, 'For me, pizza is love, colour and poetry. LOVE because it's an unconditional feeling; in Italian it rhymes with sweetness, passion and creation. It's giving your time and energy to create something that touches someone else with every bite. COLOUR because my vision of pizza takes aesthetics into account. I enjoy inventing combinations that always feature a complex array of toppings. POETRY because I play with nature and its protagonists. The ingredients should give each pizza its own distinct rhymes.'

# THE PERFECT
## *CARBONARA*

With 20,000 fresh eggs going into its *pasta carbonara* every year, Eggs has established itself in recent years as the authority when it comes to this legendary dish.

Here, organic eggs from chickens, geese, ostriches and sturgeons – all from fair-trade, sustainable farms – are transformed into flans, custards, zabaglione and, naturally, *carbonara*, which is available in nine variations.

**EGGS**
**VIA NATALE DEL GRANDE 52**

+39 06 581 7281

eggsroma.com

89

# A BISCUIT THAT WILL
# **TAKE YOU BACK**
# **IN TIME**

In a quiet corner of Trastevere, Biscottificio Artigiano Innocenti produces traditional biscuits in a delightful bakery designed around its superb 1950s oven. To go on a nostalgic trip back in time, just push open the doors to this shop run by Stefania, a fourth-generation member of the founding family.

Be sure to try one of their star biscuits: the *brutti ma buoni* ('ugly but good').

**BISCOTTIFICIO ARTIGIANO INNOCENTI**
**VIA DELLA LUCE 21**

+39 06 580 3926

# LIKE A SUNDAY
# **IN THE COUNTRY**

At the heart of the magnificent gardens of the Villa Doria Pamphili, 10 minutes south of central Rome by car, Vivi Bistrot has, ever since it opened, been offering ready-to-go picnic baskets. Pick one up at the restaurant and set out into the huge park on foot or by bike to enjoy lunch al fresco – like a Sunday in the country. Brilliant.

If you prefer not to wander so far, the terrace in the garden is superb. At night, enjoy a candlelit dinner in a former barn in the park.

**VIVI BISTROT**
**VILLA DORIA PAMPHILI**
**VIA VITELLIA 102**

+39 06 582 7540

vivibistrot.com/en/picnic-2

# A GREAT LITTLE BISTRO
## IN A FISHMONGER'S SHOP

Located about ten minutes by car from Rome's historic centre, Meglio Fresco (meaning "better fresh") is a delightful fishmonger's shop that transforms itself into a fantastic fish and seafood restaurant at lunch and dinner time.

Once the shutters of the shop have been lowered, the owners Arturo and Mary set up a few tables next to the display of the catch of the day. Here you can savour specialities like broccoli and skate soup, spaghetti with sea urchins, and Catalan-style lobster, all of it washed down with excellent wine.

A moment of true joy ...

📍 **MEGLIO FRESCO**

**Roma Boccea**
Via di Boccea 350a
+39 06 663 5411

**Roma Vigna Clara**
Via Pompeo Neri 42
+39 06 3974 4119

megliofresco.it

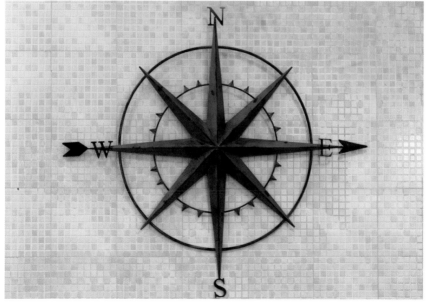

## - FULVIO PIERANGELINI -
PERFECTION MADE SIMPLE

After earning every star and charming every critic, Fulvio Pierangelini, Italy's best chef (yes, you read that right: best chef) closed his restaurant to travel around the world and helm the kitchens of the Rocco Forte Hotels group. Now, still basking in his exceptional reputation, he's back in Rome, where he runs the kitchens at Hotel de la Ville, after having taken charge of those at Hotel de Russie.

**Fulvio, your cooking smells deliciously of jasmine and oranges. But what's the flavour of Rome?**
Rome teaches the art of seduction. You learn about the flavours of its markets, countless leaves, herbs that allow you to make apparently simple everyday – sometimes even banal – dishes, but which should be made with the very feminine instinct of trusting ones senses. I'd say above all, an obsessive attention to ingredients.

**What does being born in Rome and having studied political sciences mean to you?**
While I may be Roman on the one hand, and consequently the child of multiple and complex cultural strata, on the otherI look for perfection in simplicity and openness towards the rest of the world.

I didn't travel for decades; I was afraid of flying. Today I'm constantly on the go. I'm still anchored in pasta with tomato sauce, the Parmesan in *parmigiana*, and veal tonnato, but I also play with Middle Eastern spices.

## Do you have any culinary taboos?

I don't like the banality of contemporary cuisine that feels it has to *"épater le bourgeois"* (shock the middle class) by aspiring to pointless excess. I hate terms like "deconstructed", "revamped", and "gourmet". I try to keep things simple and follow the compass of what's "good", whether I'm cooking privately for the VIPs of the world or sharing my recipes in the places I host.

## How would you describe yourself?

Dynamic, erratic, strict.

**MOSAICO**
Via Sistina, 69
+39 06 9779 3710
Daily for breakfast, lunch and dinner,
on the second floor of the Hotel de la Ville
(enter through the hotel courtyard
or banquet hall)

**DA SISTINA**
Via Sistina, 69
+39 06 9779 3710
Daily

# VISITING THE VATICAN
# **WITHOUT TOURISTS**

While there's no doubt that the Vatican Museums are fabulous, visiting them at the same time as everyone else, drowned in masses of tourists, can ruin the experience.

To visit these magical spaces in the peace and quiet they deserve, just put yourself in the hands of an expert guide, who will let you in before the doors open to the public in a group of six to eight people at most (or even for a private tour, depending on your budget ...).

For the even greater privilege of discovering rooms that are usually closed to the public, ask your guide to make a reservation to visit the Gabinetto delle Maschere or the Sala degli Animali. That's as much as we'll say.

**CONTACTS**

**Carolina Vincenti:** cvincenti@inwind.it
(Italian, English and French)
**Francesca Corsi:** francescacorsi@yahoo.com
(Italian, English and French)

**Paola Lauro :** paolalauro@tiscali.it
(Italian, English and French)

# A QUIET BAR
# **WITH A VIEW**

In Rome, pleasant terraces far from cars, scooters and tourist crowds are curiously few and far between. The one at Bibliobar, the 'book bar' right across from Castel Sant'Angelo, is perfect: here, you can enjoy a good porchetta panino, coffee, smoothie or cocktail in peace and quiet along the Tiber while leafing through the day's papers or one of the many books on the café's shelves. A moment of dolce vita that you'll relish drawing out as long as possible.

PHOTO CREDIT: LAURA SBARBORI

**BIBLIOBAR**
**FEDERAZIONE ITALIANA INVITO ALLA LETTURA**
**LUNGOTEVERE CASTELLO**

+39 340 941 9288                    invitoallalettura.org/bibliobar-bouquinistes

# THE ROMAN BISTRO
# **OF YOUR DREAMS**

Just a few steps from the historic centre, Arcangelo Dandini showcases the fabulous ancient recipes of papal Rome in a warm and friendly decor that reflects his personality.

While the food here can be elaborate, at heart l'Arcangelo remains an essentially Roman eatery, where you can enjoy the capital's major gastronomic musts, such as *cacio e pepe*, *carbonara* or the divine *polpette*.

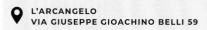 

**L'ARCANGELO**
**VIA GIUSEPPE GIOACHINO BELLI 59**

+39 06 321 0992

larcangelo.com

# JOGGING AMONG THE
## GODS OF THE STADIUM

After strolling around the Vatican Museums for hours, sometimes you're in the mood for some real sport. To go for a jog in beautiful surroundings, head over to the magnificent Stadio dei Marmi ('marble stadium'), where you can step up your pace while admiring the 64 statues dedicated to athletes that will transform a simple stroll into a theatrical experience.

Designed as the Foro Mussolini in 1928 and inaugurated in 1932 to celebrate the spirit of competition under the Fascist regime, the stadium overlooks the immaculate green of Monte Mario, the imposing mass of the 1930s-style Ministry of Foreign Affairs and, in the distance, the waters of the Tiber. *Mens sana in corpore sano* – with the added bonus of some breathtaking views.

Two other good places to go jogging near the historic centre: around the Circus Maximus and along the banks of the Tiber.

**VIALE DELLO STADIO DEI MARMI**

+39 06 324 0334
+39 331 946 7228

marmi@fidallazio.it

Free admission

# VISIT ONE OT THE MOST
# **BEAUTIFUL VILLAS**
# **IN ITALY**

Rome is full of so many wonderful treasures that it wouldn't necessarily occur to you to leave the city if you're only there for a couple of days. And yet, escaping the hustle and bustle and the crowds of tourists to discover the surrounding areas of the capital is a real treat, especially if the programme includes the fabulous Villa Farnese in the small village of Caprarola, just an hour from Rome.

Built during the Renaissance by the Farnese family, the villa (officially called the Palazzo Farnese di Caprarola) is without a doubt one of the most beautiful in the whole of Italy. Its monumental staircase (the Scala Regia) and the Room of Maps (Sala del Mappamondo by Giovanni Antonio da Varese, nicknamed the Venosino) are absolute masterpieces that would rank as the highlights of any visit.

Another great advantage of the villa is that, along with its beautiful Italian gardens, it is virtually unknown to tourists, so you can expect to be practically alone there!

**VILLA FARNESE**
**PIAZZA FARNESE 1**
**01032 CAPRAROLA VT**

visitcaprarola.it/en/luoghi-da-visitare/edifici-storici/palazzo-farnese

We never reveal the 31ˢᵗ address
in the Soul of series because it's strictly confidential.
Up to you to find it!

# A SECRET
# DRINK

Considered the inventor of the cocktail in the 19th century, today the American Jerry Thomas has lent his name to a speakeasy in Vicolo Cellini, right near Chiesa Nuova – we'll leave it up to you to figure out at which number.

But first you'll have to go to the website to get a password: you'll need to give this at the door in order to be admitted to enjoy a cocktail surrounded by the gorgeous 1920s-themed decor.

PHOTO CREDIT: JERRY THOMAS

**JERRY THOMAS**
**VICOLO CELLINI**

Many thanks to Paolo Scotto di Castelbianco for sharing his deep knowledge of Rome.

**This book was created by:**
Carolina Vincenti, author
Sofia Bernardini and Claire de Virieu, photographers
Yasmine Awwad, cover photo
Clara Mari, illustrator
Emmanuelle Willard Toulemonde, layout
Sophie Schlondorff, translation
Jana Gough, editing
Kimberly Bess, proofreading
Clémence Mathé and Roberto Sassi, publishing

You can write to us at contact@soul-of-cities.com
Follow us on Instagram on @soul_of_guides

THANK YOU

**In the same collection:**

Soul of Amsterdam

Soul of Athens

Soul of Barcelona

Soul of Berlin

Soul of Kyoto

Soul of Lisbon

Soul of Los Angeles

Soul of Marrakesh

Soul of New York

Soul of Tokyo

Soul of Venice

© JONGLEZ 2024
Registration of copyright: February 2024 - Edition: 02
ISBN: 978-2-36195-720-9
Printed in Slovakia by Polygraf